this book belongs to

_ _ _ _ _ _ _ _ _ _ _ _ _ _ _

_ _ _ _ _ _ _ _ _ _ _ _ _ _ _

_ _ _ _ _ _ _ _ _ _ _ _ _ _ _

_ _ _ _ _ _ _ _ _ _ _ _ _ _ _

Published in 2020 by
agnes & aubrey
1st Floor, Unit D,
Emperor House, Dragonfly Place
London SE4 2FL

www.agnesandaubrey.com
hello@agnesandaubrey.com

Concept, text, hand-drawn fonts and illustrations
copyright (c) 2019-20 Mary Richards

Designed by agnes & aubrey

A CIP catalogue record of this book is available
from the British Library

ISBN 978-1-9164745-5-0 (UK edition)
ISBN 978-1-9164745-7-4 (North American edition)

This edition distributed by
Consortium Book Sales & Distribution, Inc.,
part of the Ingram Content Group

Thanks to:
David, Arlo, Zubin, Quincy, and Viola Schweitzer;
Poppy Andrews, Monika Loewy, Oliver Grieb,
Becky Overton, and Megan Cabot

Printed in China
on paper from responsible sources

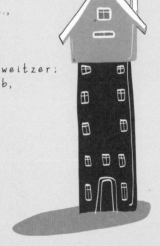

MIX
Paper from
responsible sources
FSC® C124385
FSC
www.fsc.org

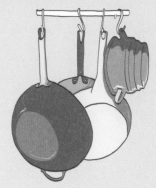

take me home

an ACTIVITY JOURNAL for YOUNG EXPLORERS

by mary richards

ALL ABOUT THIS BOOK

You can use this book whenever you are at home!
It will help you:

>> EXPLORE your surroundings.
>> CREATE and DISCOVER new things.
>> REMEMBER all the fun you've had!

The book is divided into five color-coded ADVENTURES.
You can start a new CHAPTER whenever you like - there
are no rules! You might complete one in a day, or take
longer. Throughout the book you will find FACTS about
homes and the things we put in them. There's also a
GLOSSARY at the back, to look up words you don't know.

When you're exploring your home, there are a few
important rules to keep in mind.

>> Keep safe! Don't touch faucets, power plugs, or sockets.
>> Don't explore spaces that you're not supposed to enter.
>> Ask permission from your grown-up before going to look at
the outside of your home.
>> Clean up! Always put things back where you found them.

draw your face here

Your NAME

- -

Your ADDRESS

- -

The DATE you started this book

- -

Your favorite ROOM in your home (and why!)

- -

- -

- -

A famous home you'd MOST LIKE TO VISIT

- -

THINKING ABOUT HOMES

Homes are all different. The home you live in may have been built a long time ago, or only recently. It could be made from bricks, wood, concrete, glass, or a mix of those materials. Some buildings are designed for many people to live in; others are created for a small group.

>> In the 19th century, BRICK was a popular choice for home building in many countries across the world. Between 1837 and 1901, during the reign of Queen Victoria, several million homes were built in the United Kingdom. In STREETS like this one, homes are joined together with no gaps, which helps keep them warm. Today, these large houses are often divided into separate APARTMENTS.

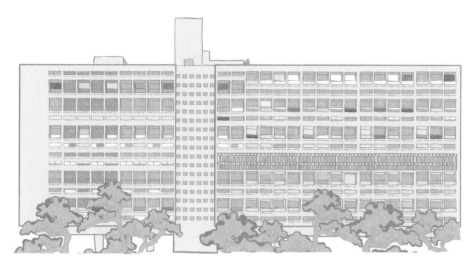

>> Designed by the Swiss-French architect LE CORBUSIER, this 18-story building in MARSEILLE, France was completed in 1952. It is made of concrete, and contains 337 separate apartments. Le Corbusier thought of the building as a "city," so he included indoor "streets," shops, restaurants - and even a roof garden with swimming pools.

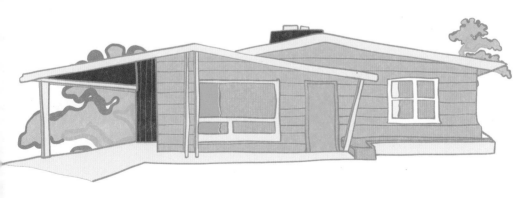

>> This American home was designed in the mid-20th century for just one family to live in. Homes like this were built to order - the buyer could choose from a number of different styles and features.

PLACES AND SPACES

Here are some unusual living spaces from around the world. Would you like to design an interesting place to live? You can draw your own "dream home" at the back of this book.

Around the world, there are many examples of homes built into ROCK or in CAVES. Thousands of years ago in Cappadocia, Turkey, homes were carved directly into its famous cone-shaped rocks. Now, some of these are hotels.

Houses designed by the Spanish architect Antoni Gaudi (1852-1926) look rather like pieces of sculpture. Casa Batlló in Barcelona, Spain has shimmering roof tiles that are designed to look like the skin of a dragon, curved balconies shaped like masks, and pillars carved to look like bones.

Houses on STILTS known as "palafitos" can be found on a group of islands called Chiloé, off the south coast of Chile in South America. The houses were designed this way so they could be moved around - sometimes homes were even put on rafts and carried across water.

FALLINGWATER, designed by the American architect Frank Lloyd Wright (1867-1959) in Bear Run, Pennsylvania was built on a waterfall, which still flows through it. He wanted the home to blend with its natural surroundings.

THINGS THAT SURROUND US

Have you ever stopped to think about the different OBJECTS that fill your home? They make the space unique, and special to you. Here are some things to look out for in your home.

>> DECORATIONS made of FABRIC like CURTAINS, CARPETS, or RUGS.

Persian rugs are famous for their detailed patterns. Carpet weaving is an ancient tradition, and some thousand-year-old rugs still survive today.

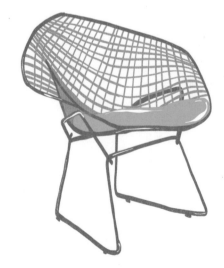

>> FURNITURE for SITTING, EATING or SLEEPING.

Chairs have changed over the years! The "diamond" chair was made in the USA in 1952 by Italian-born designer Harry Bertoia (1915-1978). It's made of steel.

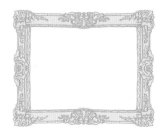

>> PICTURES OR MIRRORS ON THE WALL
Paintings and photographs make us feel at home. They remind us of people we love, and friends living in other places.

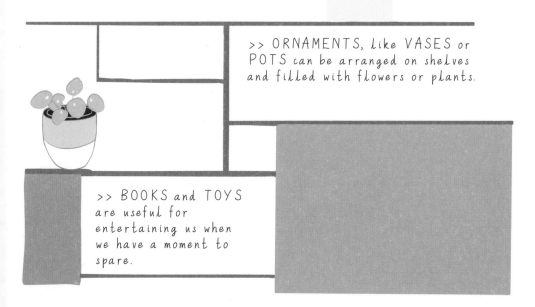

>> ORNAMENTS, like VASES or POTS can be arranged on shelves and filled with flowers or plants.

>> BOOKS and TOYS are useful for entertaining us when we have a moment to spare.

What's your favorite piece of furniture in your home?

- -

Draw the view from a WINDOW in your home. What do you see?

- -

ADVENTURE NO.1

What's the DATE?

- -

WHO are you with?

- -

What's the ADDRESS of the home you're exploring:

- -

- -

- -

WHO lives here?

- -

- -

MAP IT OUT

When ARCHITECTS draw PLANS, they imagine they are looking down on the space from above - like a bird.

Here are some of the symbols they use to describe the parts of the room or building they are designing.

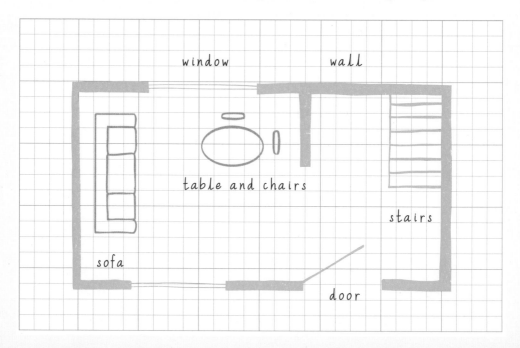

window

wall

table and chairs

stairs

sofa

door

Let's make a PLAN of the ROOM you're in! Remember to include the position of DOORS, WINDOWS, and any large pieces of FURNITURE. You can LABEL your drawing, too.

>> CIRCLE the type of room you've mapped out today:

living room   kitchen   bedroom   bathroom

other room: _

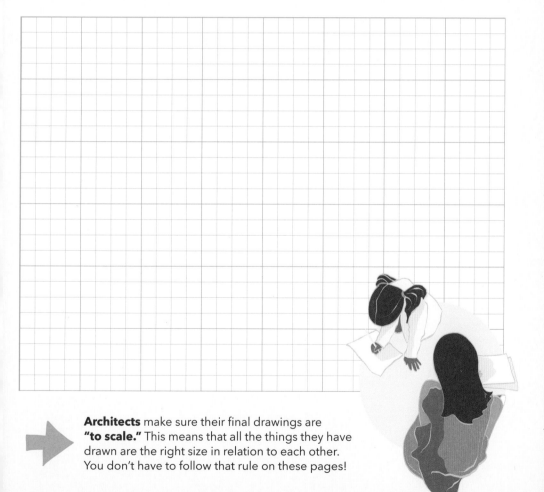

Architects make sure their final drawings are **"to scale."** This means that all the things they have drawn are the right size in relation to each other. You don't have to follow that rule on these pages!

INSIDE
OUTSIDE

ALL HOMES are different. UNDERLINE the sentences that describe your home:

>> It is in an apartment block.

>> It is in a large house that's divided into several apartments.

>> It is a townhouse.

>> It is a home on one-story.

>> It is detached - it is not connected to any other homes in the street.

>> It was built after 1900.

How many people live in your home?

- -

Homes are made from many different combinations of MATERIALS.

Look at your home from the OUTSIDE. Is it made of:

brick   glass   wood

concrete   steel   something else:

- -

>> Can you find out WHEN your home was built?
Or any other interesting things about your home?

- -

- -

- -

Can you imagine living in a home made entirely of glass? German-American architect **Mies Van der Rohe** (1886-1969) designed **Farnsworth House** with glass walls, so that its owners could see woods and fields at all times. It was built in the countryside outside Chicago in 1951.

LIVING SPACES

If we took all the FURNITURE out of our homes, most
ROOMS would look very similar. All rooms have walls,
ceilings, floors, and usually a window. The things we put
in these rooms make them look different.

>> Head to a room in your home (for instance, the
KITCHEN or LIVING ROOM). Make a note of all the
things that you can ONLY find in this space - not
anywhere else in your home:

- -

- -

- -

- -

- -

- -

DRAW your favorite thing in the room here.

This is a picture of:

- -

 Houseplants have been in homes for hundreds of years! In 17th-century Europe, home-makers were keen on bringing the outdoors in. Glass rooms filled with orange and lemon trees became very fashionable.

To grow, houseplants only need a light space (like a windowsill), some water, and occasionally a little plant food. Plants are good for the air, too – they breathe in carbon dioxide and breathe out oxygen.

HOW DOES IT WORK?

In our homes, there's lots going on that we can't see. Homes need ENERGY to power LIGHTS and APPLIANCES, and to heat the WATER in the faucets.

>> Look around you. Which room are you in?

- -

>> How many LIGHTS can you see?

- -

>> How many HEATERS are in this room?

- -

The **Romans** used a kind of **underfloor heating** to keep their homes cozy over 2,000 years ago. They built floors on raised columns, trapping heat in the space underneath. This way, they could keep their living spaces - and their famous thermal baths - nice and warm.

All about ELECTRICITY

ELECTRICITY is the flow of charged particles around a circuit. Electric CURRENTS power nearly everything in our homes - from lights to fridges.

>> POWER PLANTS make our electricity. Here are some different types.

coal, gas or nuclear

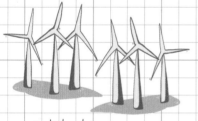

hydro-electric
(water energy)

wind turbines

>> They are all connected to a GRID of electric cables. This carries the electricity to our homes.

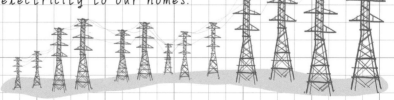

>> Some homes have SOLAR PANELS on the roof, which turn energy from the sun directly into electricity.

SLEEPING SPACES

Take a look at your BED. You could LIE DOWN on it and relax! Think of some words to describe your pillows or bedspread.

- -

- -

- -

SLEEP is very important. It's good to get ten hours of sleep every night to recharge. Did you know that:

>> Our brains are awake and working, even while we're asleep.

>> Sleep is a time when our bones grow and our bodies heal.

>> Sleep helps our brains make sense of all that's happened during the day.

>> Looking at screens in the hours before bed stops us falling asleep properly.

A comfy bed could be the key to a good night's sleep! Can you DESIGN your own bed in the space below? You might want to include some special or unusual features - which you can label on the drawing.

 Bunk beds are named after the beds found in ships' cabins. They were cleverly designed to fit lots of sailors in a small space. People were packed in tightly - there wasn't much room to sit up or stretch out.

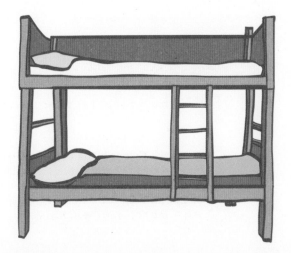

HOME STORIES

Many authors set their BOOKS inside homes. For instance, in the THE LION, THE WITCH AND THE WARDROBE (1950) by C.S. Lewis, four children enter a magical land by traveling through a closet.

>> Look around the room you're in. Pick a piece of FURNITURE. Can you plan a story around the item you have chosen? Write some ideas here.

- -

- -

- -

Now DRAW the piece in the space opposite! >>>>>>>>

In the book **Through The Looking Glass, And What Alice Found There** (1871), Alice, the hero, climbs through a magical mirror into a strange world, where everything is back-to-front – like a reflection in a mirror. Author **Lewis Carroll** may have been inspired by the huge mirror that hung in the home of the Riddell family, for whom he wrote the stories.

PICTURE GALLERY

FIND THREE OBJECTS to draw in the room you're in!
You can LABEL them underneath.

 Pop artists of the 1950s and 60s made art inspired by the everyday objects they saw all around them. This included things they found in their own homes, like food, packaging, household appliances, newspapers, and magazines.

Draw yourself waking up today. How did you feel?

- -

ADVENTURE NO.2

What's the DATE?

- -

HOW LONG have you lived in your home?

- -

What's your FIRST MEMORY of this home? Make some notes here:

- -

- -

- -

Do any PETS share your home with you?

- -

- -

MAP IT OUT

Do you use SOME ROOMS of your home more than others? Perhaps you go only into certain rooms at particular times of day?

Which room do you spend MOST of your time in?

- -

Now decide which room you visit LEAST?

- -

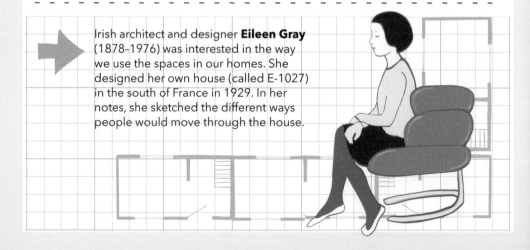

Irish architect and designer **Eileen Gray** (1878-1976) was interested in the way we use the spaces in our homes. She designed her own house (called E-1027) in the south of France in 1929. In her notes, she sketched the different ways people would move through the house.

>> Use today to RECORD how you use the space in your home. Carry this book around with you, and note down the NUMBER OF TIMES you go into these rooms. There's space to add some extra rooms, too.

living room

- - - - - - - - - - - - - - - -

kitchen

- - - - - - - - - - - - - - - -

bedroom

- - - - - - - - - - - - - - - -

bathroom

- - - - - - - - - - - - - - - -

other room:

- - - - - - - - - - - - - - - -

other room:

- - - - - - - - - - - - - - - -

Make some notes on what you found. Which room did you visit most? Did you discover anything surprising?

- -

- -

- -

INSIDE
OUTSIDE

WINDOWS let light into our homes, and allow us to look out onto the world outside. Windows facing EAST will get early morning sun. Through WEST-facing windows, you might see the sun setting in the evening.

>> Let's count the windows in your home! Ask an adult to help you work out what direction they face.

number of windows facing NORTH

- - - - - - - - - - - - - - - - -

number of windows facing SOUTH

- - - - - - - - - - - - - - - - -

number of windows facing EAST

- - - - - - - - - - - - - - - - -

number of windows facing WEST

- - - - - - - - - - - - - - - - -

>> Do you have any windows on the ceiling?
These are called SKYLIGHTS.

>> Windows come in all shapes and sizes. Choose a window in your home and draw it. You can include the view, too!

 The **windows** of a home are usually made of panes of glass or plastic. **Single paned** windows are made with just one pane. **Double or triple paned** windows contain two or three panes, with a pocket of air in between. This trapped air keeps the home extra warm.

LIVING SPACES

When you sit on a CHAIR in your home, do you ever stop to think that somebody DESIGNED it? They decided how tall its legs should be, how much padding to put on the seat, and what angle to use for the back rest.

>> Have a look around your home and make notes on TWO chairs you find there.
>> Ask yourself what the chairs are made from. How comfy are they? Do you use them for relaxing, eating at a table, or for something else?

FIRST CHAIR   SECOND CHAIR

- - - - - - - - - -   - - - - - - - - - -

- - - - - - - - - -   - - - - - - - - - -

- - - - - - - - - -   - - - - - - - - - -

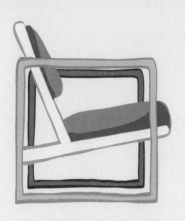

 In the 1920s and 30s a design school called the **Bauhaus** (which means "building house") was set up in Dessau, Germany. Artists and designers lived and worked together and taught classes to visiting students.

Bauhaus artists believed that furniture should look good, but also work well. Pieces of furniture, like this chair designed by Josef Albers (1888-1976) in 1927, were often based on geometric shapes – squares, circles, or triangles.

DESIGN your own CHAIR here.

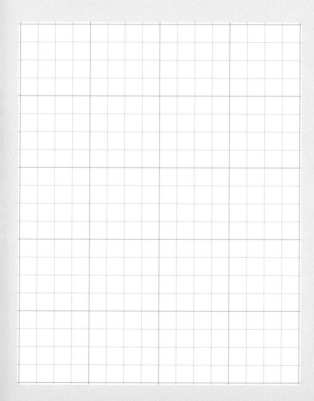

 The **Memphis Group** of designers worked in Milan, Italy in the 1980s.

They wanted to challenge ideas of what furniture should look like. Their pieces – like this table lamp by **Ettore Sottsass** (1917-2007) – were bold and brightly colored. They often combined different materials like plastic, glass, and metal, molded into exciting shapes.

HOW DOES IT WORK?

In our homes, we can turn on faucets and watch the water flow out, hot and cold. Have you ever wondered where all this water comes from?

>> Here's a list of some places in your home that you will find water.

faucets - kitchen sink   faucets - bath
faucets - shower   toilet

>> How many FAUCETS can you count in your home?

- -

>> WASHING MACHINES need water to work. Can you list any other appliances in your home that use water?

- -

- -

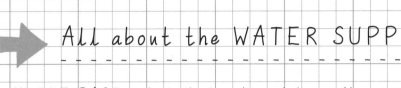

All about the WATER SUPPLY

IN THE PAST, nobody had water at home. It had to be fetched in buckets from WELLS or nearby RIVERS.

The water that flows from our faucets has a JOURNEY to take before it reaches our homes.

>> WATER TANKS and RESERVOIRS store the water that we pipe into our homes. Here, it is also CLEANED and made DRINKABLE.

>> FAUCETS control the flow of water in our homes. This water comes from PIPES that run underneath our streets.

>> In homes with CENTRAL HEATING, the water is HEATED UP by a WATER HEATER. The water is sent through the home to FAUCETS through a system of PIPES.

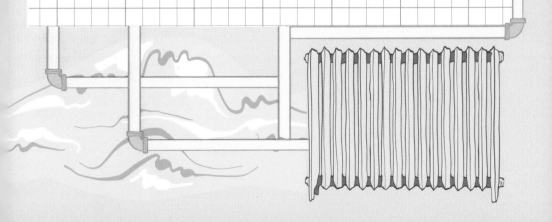

SLEEPING SPACES

BEDROOMS are for not just for sleeping. They are also for storing our belongings. These might include clothes, books, toys, crafts, and other special keepsakes.

>> Do you have a BOOKSHELF? Here are some ways to ORGANIZE your books:

by type (e.g. story books, books of facts)
by size, by color or in alphabetical order
by books you want to read next
by favorites - in order of how much you enjoyed them

>> You can also use these ideas to arrange CLOTHES, TOYS, and other things!

What are the NEATEST and MESSIEST parts of your room?

_ _ _ _ _ _ _ _ _ _ _ _ _ _ _ _ _

_ _ _ _ _ _ _ _ _ _ _ _ _ _ _ _ _

>> Draw THREE of your favorite belongings here. They can be BOOKS, TOYS, or anything else that's SPECIAL.

 The world's **oldest bed** was discovered in South Africa by archaeologists. It's believed to be around 77,000 years old! The bed was made from rushes and reeds woven together and was large enough for several people to sleep on it.

HOME STORIES

Unless your home is brand new, it probably belonged to someone else before you moved in. Can you INVENT some characters who lived in your home before you?

_ _ _ _ _ _ _ _ _ _ _ _ _ _

_ _ _ _ _ _ _ _ _ _ _ _ _ _

_ _ _ _ _ _ _ _ _ _ _ _ _ _

_ _ _ _ _ _ _ _ _ _ _ _ _ _

_ _ _ _ _ _ _ _ _ _ _ _ _ _

_ _ _ _ _ _ _ _ _ _ _ _ _ _

 In the **Tenement Museum** in New York City, you can visit the homes of immigrant families that lived in apartments in Orchard Street on the Lower East Side between the 1860s and 1930s. The apartments are furnished as they would have been at the time.

>> Draw one of your characters here.

What's your character's NAME?

- -

PICTURE GALLERY

>> It's time to draw your KITCHEN from memory!
Go to a room that isn't the kitchen, and sketch what
you can remember. You can label the drawing, too.
When you've finished, go back and see how your picture
matches up!

Draw the view from your BED here. What can you see?

- -

ADVENTURE NO.3

What's the DATE?

- -

How old will you be on your next BIRTHDAY?

- -

List THREE things you like about your home:

- -

- -

- -

Now name THREE things you'd like to change:

- -

- -

- -

MAP IT OUT

The board game CLUE was created in 1949. It's set in a mansion with nine rooms, and the aim of the game is to solve the mystery of what happened in the house.

>> Can you invent a GAME about your home? It could be as simple as CHUTES AND LADDERS or more complicated. Write some ideas here:

- -

- -

- -

 Board games have been popular since ancient times. They appear in paintings from Egyptian tombs as far back as 3,000 BCE, and the remains of playing pieces have been found by archaeologists all over the world – from Iran to China. In 17th-century Europe **games tables** were fashionable pieces of furniture. Disguised as a table, the top could be flipped around to reveal boards for cards, chess, or backgammon.

Design the BOARD for your game here. Later, you could create a version on a larger piece of paper.

What's the NAME of your game?

- - - - - - - - - - - - - - - - - - -

INSIDE
OUTSIDE

All homes have a FRONT DOOR, whether it is outside on the street or inside an apartment building.

>> Here are some very famous FRONT DOORS:

Number 10 Downing St is the home of the British Prime Minister

The White House in Washington, D.C. is home to the President of the USA

>> Draw your own FRONT DOOR in the space on the left. Remember to include a MAIL SLOT, KNOCKER, DOOR KNOB, and DOOR NUMBER (if you have them).

>> In the space on the right, design a NEW front door!

Humans have put doors in their homes for thousands of years. Ancient Romans often painted **false doors** on the walls inside their houses. These showed off their painting skills, and tricked people into thinking they could be used to leave the room! Though 2,000 years old, some of these walls decorations still survive today.

LIVING SPACES

As well as being full of furniture, objects, and things that belong to us, our homes are full of MEMORIES - even when we haven't lived in them for very long.

For this activity, take a walk around your home. In each room, note down a strong memory of something that happened there - for example, a memorable meal or even a conversation. They can be recent, or from a long time ago. Don't think about it too hard - you can write down the first things that come to mind.

 You can also use your home as a **"memory palace"** to sharpen your actual memory skills! This trick was invented by the Ancient Greeks over 5,000 years ago. They imagined walking around a particular building, stopping at different rooms on the way. They then made pictures in their minds, "putting" the things they were trying to remember in the different places. It took a lot of practise to get this right, but they used this technique to recall long lists of facts and even whole speeches.

ROOM 1   MEMORY

- -

- -

ROOM 2   MEMORY

- -

- -

ROOM 3   MEMORY

- -

- -

ROOM 4   MEMORY

- -

- -

HOW DOES IT WORK?

It's important to SAVE water and electricity.
This is good for the planet - and reduces bills, too.

You can save WATER by:

>> taking shorter showers or shallower baths

>> turning off the faucet while you're brushing your teeth

You can save ELECTRICITY by:

>> turning off the lights when you leave a room

>> making sure your washing machine and dishwasher are
fully loaded when you use them

A few modern homes save energy by being built in the ground. **Malator**, a
one-roomed home designed in 1998 by architects **Future Systems** (pictured on
the right) was built directly into a hillside in Wales. Can you imagine living there?

All about FUTURE HOMES

Today architects and engineers work to make the new homes they build as ECO-FRIENDLY as possible. These ECO-HOMES are kind to our planet - built to save as much energy as possible.

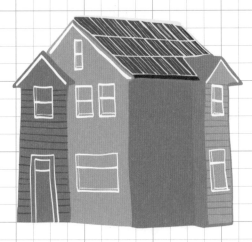

>> SOLAR PANELS attached to the roof generate all the electricity the eco-home needs.

>> The eco-home is well INSULATED to save energy; heat can't escape through its THICKLY-GLAZED windows.

>> Eco-homes are built from SUSTAINABLE or even RECYCLED materials so they do not damage the environment. This means that if they are made of wood, it has to be from forests that are re-planted when trees are cut down.

SLEEPING SPACES

Go into the room you sleep in. Look around you, and try to notice as many things as you can. Look UP, look DOWN, look on the WALLS, and look on your BED.

>> How MESSY would you say your room is today, on a scale of ONE (very neat) to TEN (extremely messy)?

- -

>> If you could CHANGE one thing about your room, what would it be?

- -

Have you ever seen a **four-poster bed**? This stylish and luxurious way for wealthy people to sleep first appeared in Europe in the 15th century. These wooden beds were raised from the floor and surrounded on all four sides by curtains - for a cozy, private night's sleep.

>> How well can you REMEMBER what's in your bedroom? Go into ANOTHER ROOM, and see how well you can answer these questions.

>> What's on the FLOOR of your bedroom? List as many things as you can remember:

- -

- -

- -

>> Describe what's next to your BED:

- -

- -

>> What does the CEILING look like?

- -

- -

>> What's on the WALLS?

- -

- -

- -

HOME STORIES

Lots of STORIES are set in HOUSES. Author Louisa May Alcott based her books, including LITTLE WOMEN (1868), on the place she lived as a child - Orchard House in Concord, Massachussetts, USA.

>> Can you think of any other stories set in HOUSES?

- -

- -

>> Plan a story of your own set at home.

First, make up an address:

- -

What's special about this home?

- -

What's the main character called?

- -

What's your story called?

- -

- -

You can DRAW something from the story here!

Mary Yelloly grew up in Norfolk, England in the 1820s. At the age of 8 she invented a story – in words and pictures – of an imaginary family she called the Grenvilles. Mary based this story (which she called a "picture history") on her own life. She created detailed drawings of this fictional family with four children, their home and their daily activities. Mary must have enjoyed the world she'd created, as she continued writing her story for four years!

PICTURE GALLERY

- - - - - - - - - - - - -   - - - - - - - - - - - - -

Find some different LIGHTS in your home and draw them on this page. You can label where they are underneath. Why not color the picture frames, too!

18th century:
CHANDELIERS
holding
MANY CANDLES

14th century:
SINGLE
CANDLES

19th century
GAS LAMP

20th century
Light with ELECTRIC BULB

Lighting has changed in our homes over the centuries. Here are some of the different lights we've filled our homes with over the years.

Find a good BOOK and draw it here! What's it called?

- -

ADVENTURE NO.4

What's the DATE?

- -

WHO is at home today?

- -

DESCRIBE what they are doing:

- -

- -

- -

WHAT are you looking forward to doing today?

- -

- -

- -

MAP IT OUT

Take a look at your KITCHEN. Circle what you find:

sink	microwave	oven
fridge	dishwasher	freezer
grill	toaster	garbage disposal

What else can you spot in your kitchen?

- -

- -

 In the gardens of **Osborne House** on the Isle of Wight, UK, Queen Victoria and Prince Albert built a small house called the Swiss Cottage in 1853, just for their royal children to play in. It had a real working kitchen, so they could test out their baking skills.

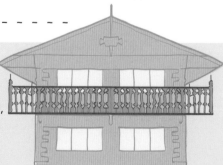

Kitchen UNITS are often made the same size so that they slot together easily. Choose a part of your kitchen to DRAW in the grid below.

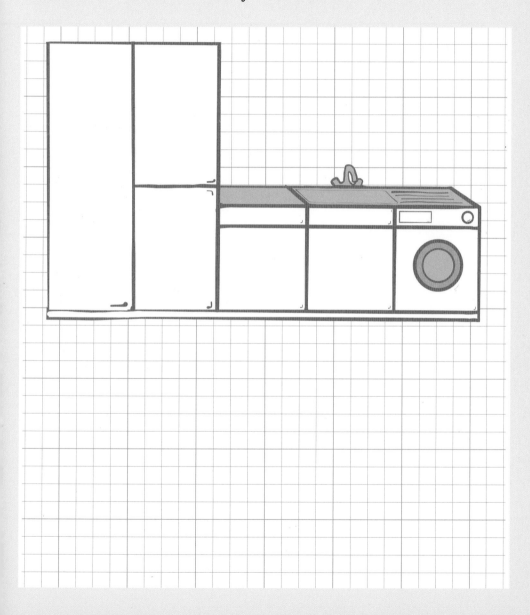

INSIDE OUTSIDE

Something connecting the inside and outside of the house is the CHIMNEY! Not all homes have one - does yours? (You won't find them in most apartments.)

FIREPLACES were important before central heating was invented - and could be found in many rooms of homes built in the 19th century.

All fireplaces were connected to a CHIMNEY - through which the smoke from the burning fuel escaped. Today, even if the fireplaces are not in use, look up and you can still see the CHIMNEY POTS - one for every fireplace in the house.

Chimneys were common in houses from the 16th century. For the next 300 years, **chimney sweeps** had to climb inside to clean the soot and ash that had stuck there. This was a dangerous job - they had to squeeze into tiny spaces full of toxic chemicals. In parts of Europe and America this job was often given to children, until this was banned in the mid-19th century.

>> DRAW a fire burning in the fireplace below. You can draw some objects on the MANTELPIECE (the shelf above the fireplace), too!

LIVING SPACES

Over the years, our living spaces have been filled with different systems for listening to music and watching moving images. Which of these do you have in your home?

- -

  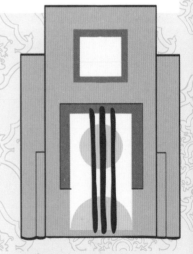

1900s:
Gramophones allow people to play recorded music in their own living rooms.

1930s:
Music and news is delivered by radio broadcasts.

1940s:
Early TVs have tiny screens, large surrounds, and don't show pictures in color.

Make a list of your favorite songs, TV shows, apps, and websites. Which devices do you use to play them?

- -

- -

- -

- -

- -

1990s:
TV sets get larger and fill living rooms.

2010s:
Games, movies, and TV shows are streamed on individual tablets and computers.

2010s:
Virtual assistants play music and respond to voice commands.

HOW DOES IT WORK?

The invention of TOILETS made our homes much more comfortable. On average, we go to the toilet around 2,000 times a year!

>> Have you ever looked closely at your toilet? Draw it here! See if you can label these things:

The FLUSH (the button or chain you use to get rid of waste)

The CISTERN (the box that holds water and a pump)

The LID (this is lifted up to open the toilet)

The WASTE PIPE (where water and waste flow out)

All about TOILETS
- - - - - - - - - - - - - - - -

Early toilets were simple holes dug in the ground, in a place away from where people lived, ate, and slept.

>> CASTLES of the 12th century were the first buildings to include toilets. There are no pipes - simply holes in the floor!

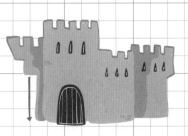

>> Toilets as we know them today didn't exist until the 19th century. Instead, CHAMBER POTS were used in homes. They had to be emptied regularly!

>> Sir John Harington (1560-1612), godson to Queen Elizabeth I of England designed a FLUSHING TOILET in the 1590s. He put one in his own home, and made one for the Queen, too. But the invention didn't catch on for another 300 years!

SLEEPING SPACES

Everyone DREAMS - it's remembering the dreams that's difficult! Most DREAMS are forgotten, but those that we do recall can be quite interesting.

Don't worry if you have a scary dream. Remember, they are not real!

>> What's the STRANGEST dream you've ever had?

- -

- -

- -

>> What would you MOST like to dream about?

- -

- -

- -

>> Keep a DREAM JOURNAL for a few days in a row.
You can leave this book next to your bed, and write in
it as soon as you wake up, before the dream is forgotten.
If it's hard to put into words, you can draw pictures!

>> FIRST DAY

- -

- -

>> SECOND DAY

- -

- -

>> THIRD DAY

- -

- -

Surrealist artists like René Magritte (1898-1967)
and Salvador Dalí (1904-1989) enjoyed painting
pictures based on their dreams. They liked the way
that you can't control what happens in a dream -
unusual stories and odd combinations of objects
just appear! Surreal means strange, or "not real."

HOME STORIES

Authors have written about HIDDEN SPACES in homes - places that you might not otherwise think about. Here are a few examples:

>> A cupboard under the stairs
(The Harry Potter series by J.K. Rowling, 1997-2007)
>> The space beneath the floorboards
(The Borrowers series by Mary Norton, 1953)
>> An old attic full of cobwebs
(The Neverending Story by Michael Ende, 1983)

Can you think of any other stories that are set in tucked away places? Make a list here:

- -

- -

- -

Now think of TWO places in your own home where stories might take place. Describe or draw them here!

FIRST "HIDDEN" PLACE:

- -

- -

- -

SECOND "HIDDEN" PLACE:

- -

- -

- -

PICTURE GALLERY

All these HOMES used to be something else. Can you think of some interesting buildings you'd like to turn into a place to live?

WINDMILL
(for grinding grain)

OAST HOUSE
(for storing grain)

WATER TOWER
(for storing water)

DRAW your ideas here! What were the homes before?

Draw your DREAM BEDROOM here! What's the best thing in it?

- -

ADVENTURE NO.5

What's the DATE?

- -

What TIME did you wake up today?

- -

What are the BEST MEALS you've ever had in
your home:

- -

- -

- -

What food do you like the LEAST?

- -

- -

MAP IT OUT

From the 16th century, DOLLHOUSES became very popular. Skilled artists made miniature versions of rich family homes and filled them with tiny objects and pieces of furniture. The first dollhouses were created for adults - it was only later that they were designed as toys to be played with by children.

A **dollhouse** belonging to **Petronella Oortman** (1656-1716) can be seen at the Rijksmuseum in Amsterdam, the Netherlands. It has nine separate rooms and large glass doors that open at the front, like a cabinet.

Petronella - a rich woman who lived in Amsterdam - spent a fortune decorating the dollhouse with silk curtains, gold ornaments and finely carved wooden furniture - exactly as if it were a real home.

Can you PLAN a dollhouse based on your own home?
This GRID might help you!

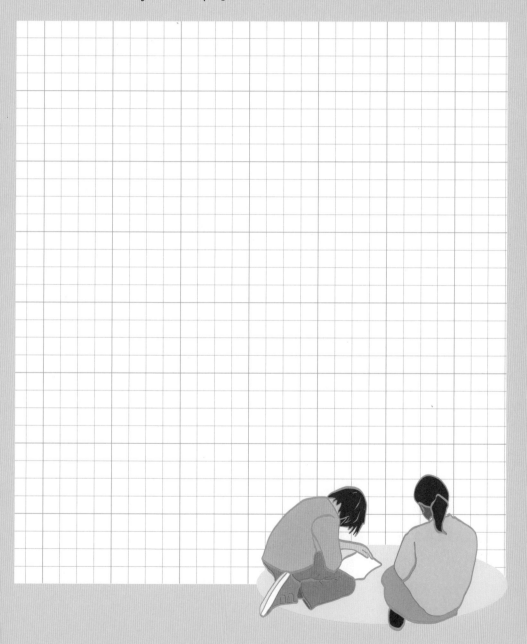

INSIDE
OUTSIDE

Does your home have any STAIRS? Why not count them!
You can include single steps and front door steps.

- -

In your home, how long does it take you to get from
place to place? Don't race! Walk at your normal speed.

>> From your FRONT DOOR, how many SECONDS does
it take you to get to your BEDROOM?

- -

>> From your BEDROOM, how many SECONDS does
it take you to get to a BATHROOM?

- -

>> From the BATHROOM, how many
SECONDS does it take you to get
to the KITCHEN?

- - - - - - - - - - - - - - - - -

STAIRS are fun to draw! Practise in this space.
There are some examples to inspire you.

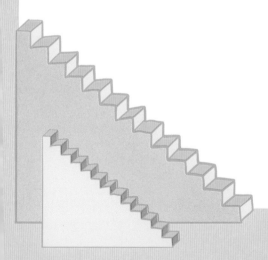

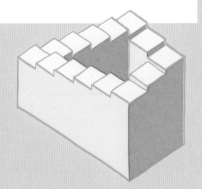

 Dutch artist **M.C. Escher** (1898-1972)
drew hundreds of staircases during his life.
Many of them were picture puzzles - optical
illusions known as "impossible staircases."
They didn't lead anywhere, but appeared to
go round and round in a neverending loop.

LIVING SPACES

The KITCHEN is one of the most-used spaces in a home. Whether it's for COOKING, EATING, or ENTERTAINING, it's a room you probably spend lots of time in.

Our kitchens are filled with GADGETS for preparing food and drink - and cleaning up afterwards! How many of these can you find in your kitchen:

coffee machine	kettle	juicer
dishwasher	water filter	scales
blender	breadmaker	whisk

 American engineer and psychologist **Lillian Gilbreth** (1878-1972) studied the way we use the spaces in our home and the objects in them. She designed inventions to improve our way of life. These included an electric food mixer, a pedal-operated trashcan, and shelves in fridge doors. She also had twelve children - and many of them helped test out her theories!

Great inventions solve a problem or make a task easier.

>> Is there a task in your kitchen that you struggle with? Write some ideas for a gadget you might create:

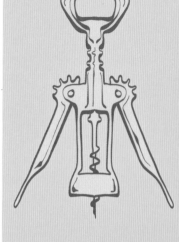

- - - - - - - - - - - - - - - - - - - -

- - - - - - - - - - - - - - - - - - - -

- - - - - - - - - - - - - - - - - - - -

>> Have a go at DRAWING your invention here!

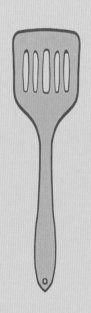

HOW DOES IT WORK?

It's important to keep homes CLEAN! Do you do any chores around the house? With your grown-up, make a list of any TASKS you might be able to do - to keep your living spaces clean, neat, and tidy. There's space to DRAW yourself doing the chores, too!

BEDROOM

- - - - - - - - -

- - - - - - - - -

- - - - - - - - -

- - - - - - - - -

BATHROOM

- - - - - - - - -

- - - - - - - - -

- - - - - - - - -

- - - - - - - - -

KITCHEN

- - - - - - - - -

- - - - - - - - -

- - - - - - - - -

- - - - - - - - -

All about CLEANING HOMES

- -

Over the years, we have invented very different ways of cleaning the places we live in.

>> BROOMS for sweeping up dirt have been used in homes for thousands of years. They were made from bundles of twigs or leaves tied together.

>> WATER cleans even better when mixed with SOAP. This was used 5,000 years ago by the ancient Babylonians, who made it by combining fats, oils and salts. It was very expensive!

>> Inside a VACUUM CLEANER you'll find a fan, powered by a motor. This works to remove air from inside the machine, creating a "vacuum" that sucks the dirty outside air in to its cleaning bag.

 The first **vacuum cleaner** was invented in 1901, and was so big it had to be pulled by a horse - its suction tube had to enter through a window! Smaller machines were soon created, including those made by American **William Henry Hoover**, who designed the first "upright" cleaner in 1926.

SLEEPING SPACES

As well as spaces to sleep, BEDROOMS can be places to make art and write stories. Did you know that these artists often worked from their BEDS:

HENRI MATISSE (1869-1954)

At the age of 80, Matisse created some of his most famous works from the bedroom of his apartment in the south of France. His "cut-outs" were made from shapes he cut from pieces of painted paper, and arranged with pins on his bedroom wall. He called it "drawing with scissors."

FRIDA KAHLO (1907-1954)

Mexican painter Kahlo is famous for the pictures she painted of herself. She created many of them from her bed in her home in Coyoacan, Mexico, using an easel made especially for her. Kahlo had been injured in an accident at the age of 18, and had to spend a lot of time at home. She put her energy into making art.

>> Sit on your bed, with a MIRROR and a PENCIL. Can you create a SELF-PORTRAIT here? >>>>>

>> Create a collage in the space below. Find some pieces of colored paper and cut them into shapes. Then stick the pictures in!

HOME STORIES

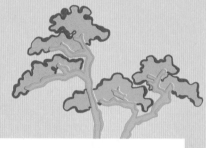

Writers and film-makers invent exciting homes for their characters to live in - treehouses, castles under the sea, pods on the moon, underground caves. . . with a bit of imagination, characters can live in amazing spaces!

>> Note down some ideas for crazy homes here.

- -

- -

- -

>> Now plan a story set in an AWESOME home space.
First, list THREE things that make it unusual:

- -

- -

- -

What happens at the BEGINNING of your story?

- -

- -

And in the MIDDLE?

- -

- -

And at the END?

- -

- -

PICTURE GALLERY

If you were to make a MUSEUM of your home, what
objects would you choose to put in it?
Find your favorites and draw them on these pages.

 Museum of the Home in Hoxton, London is in a group of fourteen houses built in 1714. They were "almshouses" – homes created especially for people in need.

In the museum, you can take a trip through time and see how people lived and furnished their homes over the centuries.

DREAM
HOME

You've finished your FIVE adventures and discovered new things about your own home!

It's time to design your DREAM HOME.

>> Where would you build your home?

- -

>> Who would live in it with you?

- -

>> What would be special about this home?
For instance, it could be next to a river or lake, or even include its own bowling alley!

- -

- -

- -

You can draw your DREAM HOME here!

>> Finally, invent an address
for your home:

- -

- -

- -

HOME GLOSSARY

Apartment - a room, or set of connected rooms, for living in. Large buildings are often divided into many apartments.

Appliance - a machine or piece of equipment designed to perform a task, for example a dishwasher or toaster.

Architect - a person who designs buildings and other structures like bridges or monuments. They make detailed plans of what they are creating.

Basement - a floor of a building that's below ground level.

Brick - a block usually made of baked clay, mostly used for building walls.

Bungalow - a home that's built low to the ground, usually on just one level.

Census - a count of all the people living in a country, which takes place every ten years. In the USA, the first census was taken in 1790; in the United Kingdom it was in 1801.

Central heating - a way of heating homes, using a hot water heater, pipes, and radiators.

Chandelier - a decorative light that hangs from the ceiling. Early chandeliers held candles; later ones held electric bulbs.

Cistern - a container on top of a toilet that holds water to create a flush.

Concrete - a mixture of stone, sand and water used for building. It hardens to form a grey block.

Cornice - a molded pattern at the top of a wall just below the ceiling. It is usually only found in homes over 100 years old.

Designer - a person who works out how to make something, using plans and drawings.

Dormer - a window that projects out of a sloping roof.

Drain - a semi-covered hole down which waste and water is taken away through a series of pipes.

Eco-home - a building designed to be kind to the environment. It is made to save as much energy as possible, so as not to release too much carbon dioxide into the atmosphere.

Environment - the air, land and water in which humans, animals and plants live.

Electricity - the flow of charged particles around a circuit. This creates an electric current, powering nearly everything in our homes – from lights to fridges.

Extension - part of a home that's been added on to the original building, creating more space.

Fitted kitchen - a kitchen made of units that slot together to save space and construction time.

Floorplan - a flat plan of the arrangement of a building, usually prepared by a designer or architect.

Gable - the triangular part of a house beneath two sides of a sloping roof.

Georgian home - a British home built during the reign of Kings George I, II, III, and IV, between 1714 and 1830.

Gramophone - an early machine for playing music, invented in the 1880s. This allowed people to listen to music in their homes for the first time.

Gutter - a pipe that runs along the edge of a roof, for collecting and draining away rainwater.

Joist - a beam made of wood or steel that supports walls, floors, or ceilings, so they can bear the heavy load of a home.

Loft - the top floor of a building, beneath the roof. Some lofts are converted into extra rooms or apartments so people can live there; others are used for storage.

Mains - the master pipe carrying electricity, water, or gas to a home.

Mantelpiece - a shelf above a fireplace that is often used to display objects and other items.

Mortgage - money loaned by a bank to someone buying a home. The bank pays the full amount for the home. The home-owner pays back the loan in monthly payments where fees (called "interest") are added.

Porch - the covered entrance to a home, leading up to the front door.

Power station - a place where energy from fuel, water, or the sun is converted to electricity. The stored electricity is connected to a grid of cables, which carry it to power our homes.

Reservoir - a large lake used to store water for use in homes. It can be natural or created especially.

Solar panels - flat tiles placed on the roof of a home or on a piece of land. They absorb the sun's rays and convert them into electricity.

Terrace - a line of houses connected together that share side walls.

Townhouse - a home of two or more stories that often shares side walls with others in the street.

Utility companies - organizations that supply homes with electricity, gas, water, telephone, or internet services.

Victorian home - a British home built during the reign of Queen Victoria, between 1837 and 1901.

Waste pipe - a tube that carries used water (e.g. from a sink or a toilet) to a drain. From the drain, it travels down another set of pipes, and is eventually cleaned in a treatment plant.

This CERTIFICATE shows that

(name) - - - - - - - - - - - - - - - -

has finished FIVE HOME ADVENTURES:

(1) -

(2) -

(3) -

(4) -

(5) -

signed

- -

date

- -